DEDICATION

To my king Jeffrey, who has always made sure I have no idea what the majority of books, articles, and public discourse on marriage are talking about – I thank you. Building with you is still the best decision I've ever made outside of saying yes to Jesus.

To my mother Deloris W. Leftridge, who has constantly encouraged and supported me – your efforts have not been in vain. You have been and continue to be my greatest mentor and coach. I thank God for allowing me to be your daughter.

To my father-in-law Albert E. Stover, Sr., I know you as the most loving, faithful and family centered man I have ever met. Listening to your stories of your late wife Carolyn all these years has been a blessing and encouragement to me. I will always remember the phone call we had days before the wedding. You told me "I raised my son, and he knows what to do. If you ever need me, you call me." You were right, and I thank you for your love and friendship.

To my tribe Savion, Ashlyn and Jaxon, thank you for your patience, love, support, and continual inspiration. You make me better, and I love you dearly. I always will.

CONTENTS

Introduction 7
1: Are You Mature? 11
2: Absolutely No One Can Fill Your God Space 19
3: Leave and Cleave 25
4: Establishing the Laws of Your Home 29
5: Room to Grow 33
6: Stay Humble 43
7: Money Matters 53
8: Children 59
9: The Bedroom Ministry 67
10: The Foundation 75
Prayer for Salvation and Baptism in the Holy Spirit 81
Appendix: Supplemental Tithing Lesson 85

Copyright ©2020 by Brandi M. Stover

Unless otherwise indicated, all Scripture quotations are taken from the *New King James Version of the Bible*. Scripture quotations marked (AMP) are taken from *The Amplified Bible*.

No part of this publication may be reproduced, stored in or introduced into a retrieval system, or transmitted, in any form, or by any means (electronic, mechanical, photocopying, recording, or otherwise), without the prior written permission of the publisher, except in the case of brief quotations embodied in critical reviews or articles and certain other non-commercial uses permitted by copyright law.

Request for permission should be directed to:
Email: info@mishayenterprises.com

MAIL: Mishay Enterprises, LLC
301 McCullough Drive, Suite 400 • Charlotte, NC 28262

Cover Design & Book Layout by Tiara Cloud (Anayah Graphics)
First paperback edition, January 2020.

ISBN: 978-0-578-63741-9

Printed in the United States of America

INTRODUCTION

In February of 2005, my life changed for the better. My friend Jeff and I finished our evaluation of each other and determined we would be better together as husband and wife. This "evaluation" was completed as we observed each other's values, actions, and work over a period of three years. Following this three-year period with intermittent conversations and interactions, we decided to date one another. We suspected we would make a great team, but it was time to determine if we were compatible. After dating for one year, Jeff asked for my hand in marriage, and we sought wise counsel on our decision to pursue marriage. All hands were on deck, including parents, friends, and pastors. It was an extremely exciting time, which I will never forget!

During our dating and engagement phase, we neither

saw stars nor little hearts floating in the air every time we set eyes on each other. We were excited but not unrealistic. I knew I was a person with my own culture, ways, and beliefs. I knew no matter how awesome I think I am, committing to and partnering with me day in and day out could be a lot for someone to sign up for. With this very realistic understanding of myself and my soon-to-be spouse, who also had his unique identity, I went in search of knowledge.

I wanted to make sure I was going to be the best wife I could be. I also wanted to protect myself against the spirit of divorce, which runs rampant in the modern-day world and church. Apart from engaging with my spiritual leaders and elders of the church, I went to the bookstore, so I could learn from other successful couples out there. I imagined that everyone considering marriage wants to study and learn from the wins and mistakes of others. Surely, the bookstore would be loaded with motivation, insight, and guidance, right?

Wrong! Within a week of my engagement as I walked up and down the aisles of my local Christian bookstore, I saw some of the most defeated titles under the sun. I wanted to be poured into and inspired by the successes of others; however, I felt as if I was being prepared for a long, hard battle instead of a partnership built to win. It was depressing to see row after row of books talking about infidelity, sexual issues in marriage, overcoming disconnections that can occur after parenthood, and every other "failure" topic.

A few positive books may have been out there, but

INTRODUCTION

their energy seemed to be generated from a "scare them straight" vantage point. I didn't want to hear that. I wanted something practical and positive, since marriage, after all, is something God created and instituted. It is not God's intention for people to present His gift as a potentially miserable experience that by happenstance may end up better for some.

After my study of "how to become depressed at a Christian bookstore," I went home and searched the internet for articles to see if something more inspiring was there. That experience showed me that most people who were married were not enjoying it. They seemed to operate primarily from a place of duty. Where were the husbands and wives who were operating in love? Where were the married couples who were reaping the benefits of God's intentions? I was sad to see marriage represented in such a monotonous manner.

As I searched, I also discovered that the majority of people talking about marriage had already been married for many decades. This is not a knock against experience in marriage as I love and appreciate the opportunity to learn from my elders. However, I also wanted to hear from my peers. How were they doing? What were the people in the fragile years of marriage when divorce is most likely doing to stay married?

At that moment, 14 years ago, I promised myself to write a simple book compiling the lessons I learned in the early stages of my marriage. My intention is to encourage

others who want to get married or are working to keep their marriages secure. This is my follow-through on that promise. By no means do I have all the answers. Marriage is built by two individuals, not the lines of black and white in a book. God knew exactly what He was doing when He instituted marriage. He understood the value it would add to our lives, societies, and the world.

Within these pages, you will get insight into what I've learned from experience and observation along the way. Perhaps you will find something worth applying to your relationship. Maybe you will discover a seed you want to sow into the relationship of a couple in your sphere of influence. In the end, we have an opportunity to stay excited and pursue the glorification of the Lord in our marriages. Let's pause and set our minds to do just that.

CHAPTER ONE
ARE YOU MATURE?

Life is seasonal, just like our world. Every activity has its time (Ecclesiastes 3:1-8). There are times to be active and times to rest, times to plan and times to execute. We have all been built with fully functioning internal clocks that help us navigate the world around us. But there is one problem: people don't mature at consistent rates or in sync with the world's "clock."

In our peer groups, we typically go through puberty around the same time. We start working around the same time. We complete our education around the same time. But what about maturation? At what point are we mentally and spiritually mature? In the natural, we may be physically

mature, possessing the looks and feelings of adult men or women, but what about the maturation of our souls and spirits? Even among peers, mental, emotional, and spiritual maturation can vary dramatically and be very individualized.

To explain this concept of maturation, consider that we are three-part beings: spirit, soul (the seat of the mind, will, intellect, and emotions), and we live in bodies (I Thessalonians 5:23). At the time we receive Jesus as our Lord and Savior, a new creature is born (2 Corinthians 5:17, John 3:3-7). This new creature is a spirit that is alive to God and has Christ's nature (Colossians 2:11, Titus 3:5-6). We were freed from the control of sin when we received Jesus and were born again (Romans 6:6). However, there is still work to do. It is the work of renewing our minds (Romans 12:2). We receive new spirits at the new birth, but our minds remain unchanged unless we do the work to transform them.

Renewing our minds involves growing up, submitting to the mind of Christ instead of our own understanding, and building our spirits to be the loudest voice we hear. Not only should we hear God's voice that speaks from within our human spirits, but we also need to submit to it (I Corinthians 6:17, John 10:27). Like children, we have to crawl before we walk and walk before we run as we mature in soul and spirit. We can know ourselves by inspecting our fruits (Galatians 5:19-23, Luke 6:43-45). The key to our maturation is learning to quiet our souls and submit to the leadership of the Holy

Are You Mature?

Spirit as He speaks through our human spirits.

Given we mature at different times, often as a result of our parenting, life experiences, and submission to the leadership of the Holy Spirit, we must allow ourselves the freedom to make major decisions such as marriage or parenthood at different times. Our intention may be to make life easier and not wait too long to pursue marriage and children. However, if we are too immature to handle these responsibilities, the Lord will not be glorified and there would be no reason to care at this point.

Our level of maturity plays a vital role in our ability to handle the requirements of marriage. If you are mature, you've already wiped out at least half of the opportunities for failure in your marriage. But if you are immature, the odds are stacked against you and your spouse. How can you identify someone's level of maturity? An easy way to do that is to assess how selfish the person is.

What do babies and toddlers do without having to be taught? They quickly grab and take, then assert that it's "mine." They manipulate people and situations to fulfill their needs and demands. Selfishness is an indicator of youthful immaturity. In the initial courting stages, this should be pretty easy to identify if you take your time and trust the evidence.

One of the worst things that has ever happened to Christian marriages is selfish people getting married. Marriage is an

example of Christ's love for the church (Ephesians 5:22-32). Therefore, we must take it seriously. Marriage is a walking testimony of God's relationship with the people He is in covenant with. The problem marriages face is that they are made up of imperfect people often from diverse backgrounds, who were created by God Himself to be unique. "Marriage is two imperfect people committing themselves to a perfect institution, by making perfect vows from imperfect lips before a perfect God" (Dr. Myles Munroe).

Trying to get two people to have a singular focus and way of operating can seem like an insurmountable task. In actuality, it's pretty easy with God. If you and your spouse follow God's commandment to love Him, "With all your heart, and with all your soul, and with all your strength, and with all your mind" (Luke 10:27), you will keep God in the center of your marriage. With God in the center, I can assure you, the battle is won easily.

If it's so easy, why do people fail so often? One reason is that a selfish person is not easily led. God will not force us to follow His lead, so selfish people don't follow God or their spouses consistently. No matter how good-intentioned they may be, selfish people's strong desire for self-preservation and advancement pushes away those in relationships with them.

Selfish people should not get married. Period. And smart people should not marry those who are selfish. I am not talking about the occasional mishaps that occur as a result

ARE YOU MATURE?

of being human. We all exhibit immature behavior or fail to appropriately manage our responsibilities at some point in our lives. I am referring to individuals who consistently display selfish behaviors.

You would think I would not have to point this out, but I must say that joining yourself to someone who is habitually selfish will be a source of continual frustration for you. You may think you have the patience to ride it out until the person matures, but that's a lie. Don't believe it! All the patience and maturity, you think you have will be up and out the door when you have to navigate your life alongside a toddler in an adult body. Selfish people are unsuitable for marriage!

You may wonder what other traits you should look for to identify selfishness in a person, including you. This can be a self-assessment or used to evaluate those you are thinking about entering relationships with (friend, spouse, etc.). Consider the following:

1. Does the person have an accountability problem?

For example, does the person use the words "they," "he/she," and "it," instead of "I" and "we" when they are in challenging situations? Typically, selfish people struggle with accountability and identifying the role they play in the situations they face. If in discussions, you notice the consistent use of these words, it may be a red flag.

2. Do you have to remind the person consistently to honor his/her word?

If the person does not follow through on his/her word, and you essentially have to police what is said by him or her to ensure it happens, this is a problem! Do you really want the dual responsibility of keeping up with your words and obligations, as well as the person's? Do you want to be a warden of sorts, keeping the order in the home without meaningful support?

3. Does this person openly talk about his/her faults and shortcomings?

I'm not talking about somebody who sits around beating up on him/herself. Low self-esteem is an inaccurate evaluation because it counters our worth and value. We are fearfully and wonderfully made (Psalm 139:14)! I'm talking about someone who is self-aware and can share an accurate self-assessment. A sign of maturity is the ability to identify our strengths and where we have opportunities for growth. If you or the person you are considering for marriage can't humbly and honestly do a self-evaluation, there is a reason for concern.

4. Does this individual ever put other people's needs in front of his/hers?

One of the key signs of selfishness is the inability to take what could be considered a loss. If your win is what I call "ugly," meaning you won but the field is littered with losses and bloodshed everywhere, then you didn't really win. To maintain peace, an unselfish person can see the potential losses required to win and will wave a flag before the battle even ensues. Unselfish people pick and choose what wars to wage by taking factors other than their own egos and needs into consideration.

5. Can you see the love of God operating in this person's life on a regular basis?

Does this person struggle to forgive or seem to always be mad at someone? Do not be naïve enough to think you are safe and won't soon be on that person's list of wrath. Plenty of opportunities will arise for you to strike a nerve when you get married. Do you want to spend the rest of your life with someone who is quick to cut people off as a defense mechanism or out of anger? Unselfish people give of themselves for the betterment of others. Part of how we give of ourselves is allowing God's love to flow through us to others (Romans 5:5), even when those people are not lovable.

We can ask ourselves many questions. If you have to ponder whether someone is selfish, then he/she probably is. It's not hard to identify selfishness in ourselves or others. As born-again believers, we can tell if we are selfish and lacking maturity by our resistance to following God's instructions.

If you are considering getting married to a selfish person – you have been warned. Combining your life with another person's is challenging enough without throwing immaturity and selfishness into the mix. If you are trying to love someone who only focuses on self-interests, you should explore the

root of your need to love people who are prone to hurt you. It may not be easy to hear, but people who choose to love those who are not mature enough to receive that love are doing so because of their unhealed wounds.

A selfish person is incapable of receiving you properly. The devaluation of your efforts over time will create an open door for Satan to walk right into your marriage and have a field day with it. Do you feel as if you are on the clock and time is running out for you to start a family or build a successful relationship? Do you have a deep relationship need that has been unmet for an extended time and now you are willing to settle to meet it?

From observation, many of the marriages around me (yes, the Christian marriages) that have been dropping like flies have a recurring theme: selfishness in one or both partners! Many people have tried and failed to make relationships work with individuals who should never have been trusted with another person's life and love. Value yourself enough to remain alone before you choose potential misery and grief by partnering with a selfish person. Take your time. Be real about what season you are in and focus on your maturity before ever considering marriage.

THE NOOK

Are you enjoying *Marriage is Amazing*? Scan this QR code to continue the conversation on this topic. Join Brandi and Jeffrey on "The Nook" vlog!

Chapter Two
ABSOLUTELY NO ONE CAN FILL YOUR GOD SPACE

God is the one who fills and completes us (Ephesians 1:22-23, AMP). People try to fill God's space with all kinds of things: entertainment, food, accomplishments, as well as love and affection from other people. Every person interested in marriage must learn how to identify the difference between basic relationship needs that a spouse can fill and deep-seated hunger that only God can fill.

Let's look at a couple of examples to determine the differences between a reasonable desire for your spouse and a hunger for God. If we haven't spent much time listening to our spirits, we can confuse these feelings and cross them up.

When you get married, there is a basic set of relational needs your partner should be able to satisfy. Your partner should be expected to spend reasonable amounts of time with you. By reasonable, I mean you should not expect your partner to sit on the phone with you for hours daily or to spend a string of hours with you all at once every day.

Take into consideration the demands that employment and parenting put on your spouse. Work with your spouse to identify what reasonable looks like for each of you. Be specific because you may think an hour is reasonable, but your spouse may believe spending five hours is reasonable. Communicate your expectations clearly to avoid confusion. A lack of understanding can create unnecessary frustration.

Your spouse should connect with you physically and emotionally, as well as encourage and support you. Again, what each spouse needs to feel satisfied in these areas varies. I recommend you and your spouse read The Five Love Languages, which is a very helpful resource for couples who want to learn how to communicate effectively. You can discuss what you have learned and try to apply it to your lives. Speaking in a love language that is inconsistent with how your spouse feels and receives love will open an unnecessary door to frustration. Communication is always the key. However, the level at which a spouse can connect with you pales in comparison to the level God can connect with you. Expecting a God-level connection from another

ABSOLUTELY NO ONE CAN FILL YOUR GOD SPACE

human being is fruitless.

A root cause of some people's thirst in their relationship with God is that they only explore it on a spiritual level. They do not tap into the practical and functional side of a fully developed relationship with God. God is just as interested in connecting with us about natural things as He is spiritual things. He is interested in what you decide to wear, eat or do in any given day. He will commune with you. Without His communion, you will be left wanting and seeking someone to fill this space. No matter how awesome your spouse is, he/she will fail you. By design, God's shoes are impossible to fill.

Does it drive you crazy when your spouse or the person you want to marry spends time with people other than you? Does your spouse decompress after a long day by being alone or in the company of a friend? Does that anger you? I am not referring to a neglectful partner. I am speaking about someone who enjoys other things and people besides you. Depending on your partner's personality and temperament, he/she may need space and quiet time to rejuvenate.

If you find yourself consistently frustrated or even angry because of your partner's inability to meet a deep, almost insatiable need you have for contact and communion, then your issue may be spiritual. You may have a spiritual thirst, which you unrealistically want your partner to quench. Spiritual thirst can be mistaken for other forms of hunger if you are not sensitive to your spirit. You should be aware of

the signs of spiritual thirst, not only in yourself but also in others, so you do not get caught up in the roller coaster of trying to satisfy what only God can.

I have been able to identify spiritual thirst in my life in a couple of ways. First, I realized that even though my partner was spending reasonable amounts of time with me, I was annoyed when someone or something else caught his attention. The Lord has taught me that at those times, my spouse is often getting too much of my focus. Somehow, I have taken my eyes off God, and I am zoning in too much on my spouse. If our basic relational needs are taken care of, we shouldn't be moved by the normal highs and lows of timing in a relationship. Becoming too easily disturbed and potentially critical of your spouse can be a sign you are not taking the time to fill up in the presence of God at the rate you need to.

Sometimes, your normal praise/worship/study routine will work. Other times, you need to bathe yourself in God's presence aggressively and continually. Recognizing these times will be the key to maintaining the appropriate balance in your marriage relationship. Unusual frustration and irritability can denote hunger and thirst. This is something only God can get to the bottom of with your cooperation.

Second, if I feel lethargic and have a bit of internal "blah" going on, I recognize it as a spiritual thirst. It means I am not spending enough time in the presence of God. Sometimes

Absolutely No One Can Fill Your God Space

when you are in this rut, you may look to the people around you to fix it. But they can't. Only God can fill the space in us that keeps us inspired, motivated, and moving forward. We can be assured that spiritual thirst will show up quickly if we have gotten our priorities out of order, and God is too far down the list. It can be spotted within our attitudes and relationships with other people.

If you notice you are exhibiting the signs of spiritual hunger and thirst, you must prioritize your time with God. Doing so, even at the expense of spending time with others, will improve the quality of your time overall. There is nothing worse for spouses than trying to be something they can't be or attempting to fill a need they can't fill. We have the responsibility to determine if we are being reasonable with our expectations or whether we need to go to God our Father, instead of our spouses.

Chapter Three
Leave and Cleave

At least 50% of the marriages I have watched fail did so because someone in the marriage was still holding on to someone or something other than his/her spouse. Your spouse is second only to God. Absolutely, positively, no one else should come between a married man and woman. Of course, I am not referring to situations of abuse or when lives are being threatened. In such cases, help must be sought. Otherwise, do not open the door and allow anyone to intrude and interfere with your marriage. "Therefore what God has joined together, let not man separate" (Mark 10:9). The key word here is "let," which according to Merriam-Webster Dictionary means "to give opportunity to or fail to prevent."

God wouldn't have said "let" if married people did not have the ability and authority to stop those around them from interfering with their marriages. In fact, He would not have used the word if people or circumstances would not try to intervene, to begin with. You have the ability to determine the access people have to your marriage.

I have never understood people who sit around talking about the details of their marital relationships as if it belongs to an open forum. I have also never understood married people who negatively speak about their spouses as if they had no choice but to marry them. Those who can't say anything positive about their spouses tell me more about themselves than their spouses. I'm not looking at the criticized spouses. I'm looking at the spouses who chose them!

Keep your business to yourself unless you are being counseled by a trained minister you can trust. Beyond that, you and Holy Spirit need to partner to get what you need. You may attempt to soothe your emotions by venting about your spouse but doing so exposes your marriage to danger. Some people seize the opportunity to prey on the weaknesses and faults of others. When you vent, you expose your spouse and open a door into your marriage. You could also end up with friends and relatives who refuse to forgive your spouse when you have long done so and moved on.

Women have a reputation for talking too much and perhaps that has been earned. However, men need to keep

Leave and Cleave

their mouths shut too. This is a two-way street. We may have more women than men in our population, but I can assure you a quality woman is not that easy to come by. Solomon reminded us of that fact (Proverbs 31:10). Don't forget; he spoke from a place of insight and wisdom given to him by God. Do not get caught sleeping. Know the intentions of those around you. The same good woman you are complaining about (extra ten pounds she has gained and all) may be just what your friend is looking for. Be careful!

When you venture into marriage, make sure you cut the umbilical cord with your parents. This sounds severe, but I am assuming you understand this does not mean you are to stop communicating with them, visiting or honoring them. What this does mean is to stop running decisions by them unless your spouse approves. Stop receiving their financial support and never pitch your spouse against them or vice versa.

For example, you and your spouse want to spend Christmas at home this year. Instead of telling your family you won't be attending, you say, "My wife wants to stay home for Christmas this year." Any decisions made in your home should be presented as joint decisions, no matter which partner came up with the idea. Be a united front with your parents, friends, children, and everybody else!

If the person you are considering marrying seems incapable of standing on his/her two feet, this will exacerbate

in marriage. If the person is slow to offer you support in challenging familial situations, don't expect a marriage ceremony to clear everything up. Openly and honestly communicate what you expect leaving and cleaving to look like in your home. Agree in advance. When in doubt, talk only to God and your spouse.

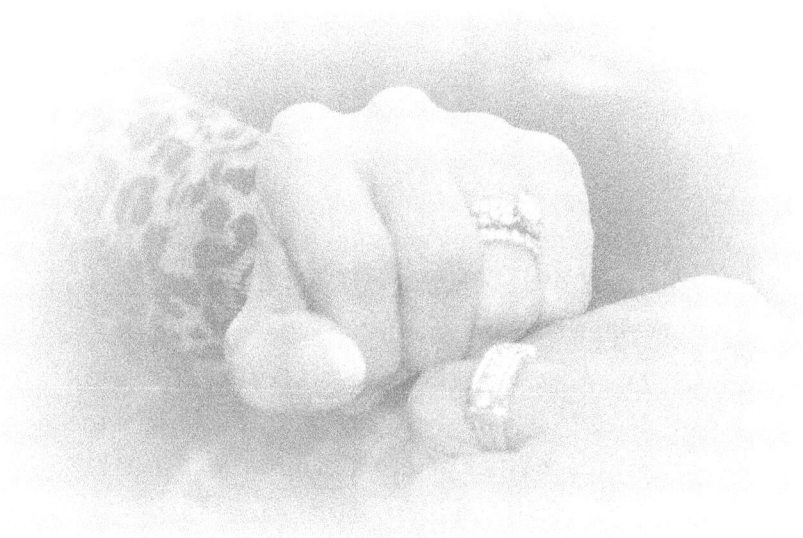

Chapter Four
Establishing the Laws of Your Home

Yes, I said laws. This means there are penalties for breaking them. People who are lackadaisical in their approach to governance in their homes end up struggling to repair the damage done. The family constitution and laws are practical agreements that must be made at the outset of your marriage. If you missed this step, by all means, do it now. It will save you a lot of drama later because you and your spouse would have already set the ground rules for day-to-day living in your home.

What works for each couple will vary, but to give you some ideas, I have shared a few laws my husband and I

verbally agreed on at the outset of our marriage. They have served us well.

1. God first, spouse second.

2. Our close friendships are same-sex and these friends are also married. We connect with other couples and not in one-on-one opposite-sex relationships.

3. Friends of the opposite sex who existed prior to our marriage were introduced to us. They either established their friendship with each other or the relationship ended. We did not drag opposite-sex friendships into the marriage.

4. Someone of the opposite sex who is not an immediate relative cannot stay in our house without the spouse being present. For example, if my husband's friend wants to come by, he needs to come at a time when my husband is at home. This is a basic safety tip too.

5. If we disagree with each other, we will do it privately and hear each other out. Regardless of what we decide, we agree in public – no lone rangers.

6. We do not permit divide and conquer tactics from our children or anyone else. We are swift to call out these tactics regardless of who is deploying them.

7. We will always assume the best of each other. If what either of us says can be interpreted in two ways, we choose to look past the delivery of the message and hear the heart of the message.

8. We do not make decisions beyond the minute level

ESTABLISHING THE LAWS OF YOUR HOME

without each other.

It's not enough to just establish the governing laws of your home; you have to actually follow them. It's largely an exercise in self-control. You will find by sticking to your agreements with your spouse, you will create a peaceful home environment that doesn't breed unnecessary conflicts.

Aside from creating the laws or ground rules in your home, you need to discuss what should happen when they are broken. This becomes especially important when you add children to your family structure. In our home, we give each other a lot of mercy but the laws are non-negotiable without prior discussion and approval by both parties. If this sounds too serious to you, consider how serious it is to sow unnecessary discord in your marriage by violating your spouse's agreements with you. It's better to err on the side of caution and respect than to frustrate and deplete your spouse over time.

THE NOOK
Are you enjoying *Marriage is Amazing*? Scan this QR code to continue the conversation on this topic. Join Brandi and Jeffrey on "The Nook" vlog!

Chapter Five
Room to Grow

Some couples are not doing well simply because they are holding each other hostage. These couples may be newlyweds or many years into their marriage. Time in the relationship has little to do with the creation of a hostage situation. Spouses who resist change, become rigid and desire excessive control create these situations.

Holding a spouse hostage can be evidenced in a variety of ways, but the root is a strong resistance to change. Often, these spouses do not support individual growth, they view it as detrimental to the marriage, rather than an asset. Individual growth is an important part of every person's life. God thinks so highly of it that even after people get

married, He maintains an individual relationship with each partner in the marriage. "And I will ask the Father, and he will give you another advocate to help you and be with you forever— 17 the Spirit of truth. The world cannot accept him because it neither sees him nor knows him. But you know him, for he lives with you and will be in you" (John 14:16-17). God values individuality; we should too. In His wisdom, God created us with distinct purposes. Therefore, marriage partners should choose to serve God as teammates, rather than be void of their individuality.

Spouses who hold their partners hostage, often lack development in areas of their lives that they have not addressed. The changes in their spouses now require they meet these development areas head-on. For example, a spouse's hobbies and interests may change. Your partner who once loved to join you on camping trips could now prefer the comfort of resorts. Mature spouses would willingly adjust how often they expect their spouses to attend these trips. They may also pursue a few camping buddies who enjoy the activity as much as they do. However, spouses who are prone to create marital hostage situations will likely complain instead of find solutions. They may even go so far as to create ample camping opportunities that no one, including themselves, will enjoy. This is because the activities are being done out of compulsion instead of genuine care.

Our partners' clothing and hairstyle preferences may

change. Your spouse who used to spend hours in the beauty salon tending to her long hair, may decide to get a short, easy hairstyle to maintain so that time could be spent elsewhere. Hopefully, the couple will discuss the matter and support each other through the process. However, partners who like hostage situations will want things to stay the same at the expense of their partners' needs.

Professions and careers may change. You may have married a doctor who chose the profession to please his/her parents. Now your spouse has matured and pleasing people is less of a priority. Your spouse may be more interested in a profession that aligns with divine purpose. Again, the couple will need to work together to process and endure this change. However, if this couple is prone to creating hostage situations, they may avoid the hard work. They will resist the changes that could ultimately lead to greater fulfillment in their marriage.

At times in the marriage, our spouses may simply outgrow us. This is especially possible if one partner in the marriage is aggressively pursuing overall wellness: physical, mental, and spiritual health, while the other is not. Spiritually speaking, the Word of God is a superfood. A person who consistently consumes the Word of God can grow into a weighty spiritual partner unable to thrive in the same old environments.

Where our spouses could once dwell in tiny "spiritual houses," they are now so large they're smothering their

spouses. An example would be a couple who at the beginning of their marriage attended church occasionally. But after God's fire was lit in one partner's life, he/she attends church every Sunday and Bible study weekly, while the other stays at home. When the partner who attends church occasionally comes home in the evening, Bible teachings are consistently playing on the living room stereo. If that partner becomes agitated and annoyed by this new environment, it's a clear sign one has outpaced the other.

Even beautiful changes like spiritual growth can shake the very foundations of a marriage if both parties are not ready to address it. It's dangerous to assume your partner can't or won't outgrow you in some area of the marriage at some point in time. The goal is to keep communicating and set levels to ensure each partner is allowed to grow while building a strong marriage.

Accepting change now puts us in a position to embrace it, and love our partners through it. Hopefully, our spouses are changing for the better and growing more into the image of Christ. Either way, we have committed to being there through it all. Not only should we be there, but the attitude we display while being there can also glorify our God. Since we know things will change, we should consider creating relationships that are built to last. Focusing on our values and compatibility with our spouse becomes all the more important.

In the book entitled The First Fifteen Minutes: For Those Dating With Marriage in Mind written by Jay Hewlin, the concept of zoning (the 15-minute process of determining your level of compatibility with others) is introduced. During our premarital counseling days, Jeffrey and I found this book to be really interesting, and it answered several questions about our overall compatibility. Within the book, compatibility is discussed in terms of a stoplight. Of course, the color red represents people who are super challenging and green represents those with whom you have maximum compatibility. Check out this book for a fun and interesting read that has served our marriage well.

In considering compatibility, I want to point out that when you get married, you do not marry the person's spirituality or gifts. You marry the entire person. When you are in the presence of a spiritually strong individual, it's attractive because that person commands and changes environments. This confidence can be attractive but don't get sidetracked.

You do not marry the way your spouse prays, worships or ministers. These are external factors that come as a result of a person's knowledge, skills, talents, and abilities. As a spouse, you will benefit from and enjoy your partner's attributes, but you are not marrying the attributes themselves. You are marrying another human being you will have to live and engage with, in the natural, day in and day out. In marriage, you are choosing to connect to who someone is. Who the person is won't always be evident by how he/she makes you feel.

As an example, let's look to God Himself. As His children, we get to enjoy His wisdom, goodness, power, and authority. We see Him demonstrate Himself in amazing ways in our

personal lives and corporate worship. We get to see Him heal, speak a word through a brother or sister, tangibly shift the atmosphere in a room, perform miracles, and other outward expressions. These are wonderful experiences, but when we are not in the midst of one of these outward expressions, do we enjoy God's presence?

Do we love Him just for who He is regardless of how we feel? Do we distance ourselves from God when His actions don't excite us or make us comfortable? What about when He challenges us or if we consider what He says a hard saying? Are we like the disciples in John 6:60-68 who stumble and are willing to walk away? When the same attributes that create the expressions we admire also create opportunities for us to be challenged, do we turn away? Jesus' spirituality was greatly reverenced and admired when all the people were receiving what they wanted. When that same anointing required people to adjust, many fell away. Those people were joining Jesus because of what they could grasp externally. They failed to connect with the man Himself.

Some Christians may feel isolated as if they don't have enough options for suitable Christian marriage partners. As a result, they can get overly excited when they see another believer's spirituality on display. Too much value can be placed on the way people pray and minister, with too little emphasis being placed on the desire for the person alone. I have seen firsthand what can happen when people get excited to have found a man or woman of God. They run speedily into marriage only to find spiritual attraction is not enough to sustain a healthy marriage.

No matter how spiritually attractive someone is, make sure you are compatible with the person if you want to commit your earthly life to him/her. If there is one area of your life you don't want to intentionally make hard, it's your marriage. Your marriage will underpin every other facet of your life. Consider:

1. Are you equally yoked? That doesn't mean just being saved; it also means being on the same spiritual level.

A yoke is a harness typically made of wood or metal. When working with oxen or other animals, you fit the yoke around the animals' necks to keep them treading together and sharing their workload. The yoke attaches to a plow or cart and distributes the pressure of the work across a team. God is always careful to give us practical examples to help us understand spiritual concepts. During the time the Bible was written, society was agrarian and nearly everyone was well-versed in what it took to keep a farm, vineyard or care for animals. These individuals knew a yoke signifies servitude and carrying the burden of a mission or task with a partner.

2 Corinthians 6:14 is speaking specifically about believers not being yoked (or joined to complete a mission) with unbelievers. However, you should also consider if the

results are any different when mature believers connect with immature or baby Christians. If you have a field to plow, would you unite a 600-pound animal with a much younger and smaller 200-pound animal? Of course not! The height difference between the animals could cause one to choke the other as the largest animal drags the other across the field. Or, the larger animal may slow down to accommodate the weaker animal and the task that should have taken a day may take weeks. Either way, you end up with an inefficient use of time and effort. If you are a spiritual giant considering connecting to a malnourished believer, you may crush the person or have authority issues in the home as a result. This is especially the case if the woman is strongest. A spiritually strong believer cannot be minimized enough to accommodate a spouse who is a baby Christian.

2. Do you have similar educational backgrounds or, at least, value education to the same degree?
3. Are you physically attracted to one another? Do you want to be seen in public together?
4. Do you have the same values? Shared hobbies are nice, but the bigger indicator of compatibility is shared values.
5. Do you feel you always have to explain away things about the person when you are around others? That will get old fast if you marry him/her. You should be able to present your spouse to the public freely and

without fear.

Do not fall into the trap of thinking you are so spiritually mature you can have a successful marriage with anyone. Can you make it work if you are being led by God and your spouse is too? Sure, I believe you can. Yet, why make life harder than necessary just for the sake of it? Use God's Word, your intellect, and heart to make sound choices. God gave you access to the total package for a reason.

Don't forget; birds of a feather flock together. Chickens and eagles trying to spend their lives together will struggle in that arrangement. There will always be a persistent battle of wills and the difference in perspectives will be tremendous if you marry someone you are not compatible with. Be smart and find someone who is more compatible because that person will be easier to serve in marriage.

THE NOOK
Are you enjoying *Marriage is Amazing*? Scan this QR code to continue the conversation on this topic. Join Brandi and Jeffrey on "The Nook" vlog!

Chapter Six
Stay Humble

We are living in a time where independence is king. Though independence is necessary for some situations, it is largely antithetical to the Christian walk as we are to be wholly dependent on God and interdependent on our spouses. The Word of God teaches us to humble ourselves (James 4:10), meaning this is something we can do. Couples need to find ways to remind themselves throughout the day, of the humility they should walk in with their spouses. After all, marriage is not like any other relationship. It is of the highest order, so we must have a servant's heart toward one another.

I remember the first time I was exposed to what real honor looks like. I was at a corporate function with over three hundred people in the room. When we entered, there were beautifully decorated tables set for a meal. I noticed that in the room, some people had placed their coats or personal belongings on the seats but absolutely no one was seated. Everyone remained standing and talking casually.

At some point, someone entered the room from the front. It caused a little stir. I watched as this person was greeted and welcomed with handshakes on entering the room. This individual, whom I soon recognized as our chief executive officer, mingled a little while. During this time, the shoes I was wearing were starting to hurt a little, but since no one was seated yet, I continued to stand too.

After about ten minutes the CEO went to the front of the room where he was surrounded by other individuals of high rank within the organization. Everyone continued to chat casually. It was not until the CEO pulled out his chair and was seated that his team also took their seats. Once this occurred, it was almost like someone started a wave at a sporting event. All around the room, people quickly took their seats.

I learned something valuable that day. There is a way to behave around and treat the people you honor. Honor is not just an internal emotion; it can be observed in a person's actions as well. I learned there are demonstrable ways to express our humility and honor for other people. I was willing to stand up for a while in honor of a man at a corporate event because of his position as CEO. My feet ached, but I stood there, showing respect for a man I didn't know personally. Furthermore, I did not select him for that position. Surely, if I can do that for him, I should show greater honor to the man I chose to be the king and priest of my home whom I said yes to.

When I was a little girl, the most successful marriage I was exposed to was that of my aunt Jo Ann. My aunt and her husband seemed to love and care for each other genuinely. They appeared to be enjoying their marriage to one another from what I could tell. Since I hoped to have the same thing one day, I would observe my aunt's interactions with her husband. One thing I noticed was she always prepared his plate before meals. Even if it was a buffet line, he would be seated, and she would enjoy preparing his plate and bringing it to him. I mentally tucked this into my mind as it seemed like a really nice thing to do. One day, in my own marriage, I planned to try it.

Fast forward – it's 2006, and I am now married. I am at a family gathering with my husband's side of the family. We've said the blessing and my husband is doing his usual talking and having a good time. I head over to the buffet table and start to prepare a plate for him. Before he is done talking, I set him a place to eat, set down his meal, and get his drink. I then let him know his meal is ready whenever he is and head back in line to get my meal.

Then out of the blue, I heard my father-in-law shout from across the room, "Now don't you start something you're not going to finish girl!" In other words, don't start this unless you want this to be something you keep up. I told my father-in-law (who I love dearly and consider a real friend) he didn't need to worry. I would keep it up. When I returned to the table, the looks I received from some of the other women in the room were quite comical. As far as they were concerned, I had just let Jeff wipe his feet all over me.

To prove a point, some people made sure I saw them get in line, together, to prepare their plates. At that moment, I could have become embarrassed by the scene, but I wasn't. I had already made up my mind what I would do, and I was committed to it. Sometimes, in the beginning, Jeff would say, "Baby, you don't have to do that. I can get it." I would just remind him – like I did everyone else – "If I am present, I prepare your plate. Now have a seat."

I am very self-aware. I know myself. I was raised by a strong single woman with no male influences in the home. The spiritual leader of my family, the matriarch, was my grandmother, not my grandfather. In general, the women who surrounded me were executives, leaders, influential, and prospering. On the outside, they did not seem to miss a beat about the fact they were single, widowed, divorced or married to men who had no desire to lead their homes. I knew that being raised in this kind of environment contributed to my

STAY HUMBLE

independence and being unafraid of succeeding in life.

I managed a team of nine people by the age of twenty-three, owned my first home by the age of twenty-four, and the list goes on. Though all of this was a direct result of God's grace, and I knew full well I was just the instrument He was using to demonstrate Himself, I knew I needed to build guardrails into my marital relationship. I had to do this because of how God has chosen to use me in leadership roles in every area of my life since childhood. I wanted consistent reminders that at home, I would now have a leader, Jesus would use to guide our family. My job is to serve at my husband's side as his helper.

That doesn't mean my husband doesn't serve me because he does, and he does it extremely well. However, I knew if we did not build things into our relationship – no matter how simple – to remind us of the role we play in each other's lives, we would be more susceptible to problems down the road.

Think about what you will do to remember your spouse is not just an ordinary person in your life. Your husband or wife is not just your associate or your roommate but a person of honor in your life. What will you do to demonstrate your honor? The Word of God teaches us to be completely humble, gentle, and patient with one another (Ephesians 4:2). How will each of you stay humble and build mechanisms in your home to serve one another?

Humility is demonstrated through our actions. Humble

people are willing to serve in unappealing ways if necessary. In John 13:1-17, we see the account of Jesus washing His disciples' feet. During this time in history in the Mediterranean region, the popular footwear was sandals. On the streets, with feet partially or completely exposed, one would encounter dirt and animal droppings. As a result, foot washing became a natural part of daily life, much like how we bathe.

The Creator of the universe went around a room, physically lowered Himself to the ground, and held the dirty and smelly feet of His disciples one by one. He thoroughly washed the dirt and grime that had accumulated on their feet and between their toes since the last time their feet had been washed. The act of washing feet was considered such a low task that one of Jesus' disciples couldn't stand the thought of allowing Jesus to serve in this way (John 13:8). What did Jesus desire us, His disciples, to learn from His actions? In John 13:12-17, Jesus explains that if He, our Lord, is humble and serves, going so far as to do the dirty work, then we too ought to do the same for one another.

In our marriages, the institution that expresses God's relationship with the church (Ephesians 5:21-33), we have an amazing opportunity to demonstrate our honor for one another and to glorify God in the process. Husbands and wives need to consider meaningful ways to show honor to each other. For example, take a behind the scenes look into

Stay Humble

our home:

- Before agreeing to go somewhere or do something outside the home, Jeff and I have a discussion to be sure we don't have anything to be done in our home that is more important at that time. Do we need some time alone as a couple? Does one of us need some time to meet the needs of a particular child? We ask for and receive each other's counsel on what is most important. We give our time and energy to each other before we commit it elsewhere.
- We navigate our careers as a couple. Whenever a new opportunity comes up, we review it together and one of us has the final say. I remember when I was up for a major promotion. On the outside, it was a no brainer. Yet, I made sure my manager knew I would discuss it with Jeffrey and come prepared the next day with any questions we may have. Helping those around you understand you do not act alone and there is shared authority in your home is an act of humility and honor. When Jeffrey was ready to change employers, he let me know, and we agreed before he moved. We ensure people understand that when they engage with one, they engage with both, and we don't move without the other's consent.
- We have practical ways we serve each other domestically. In our home, the determination for who gets the task is based on time and skill, not cultural norms.
  ➢ I drop the children off at the bus stop each morning,

and Jeff gets the children off the bus each afternoon.
- We share grocery shopping duties.
- Jeff is the family homework coordinator; I am the family schedule coordinator.
- I research and get the children involved in extracurricular activities, and we work together to get them to and from those activities.
- We work together to set the household budget. Jeff administers it and makes sure everything is paid.
- Jeff manages the children's dentist appointments. I manage the children's doctor appointments.
- I coordinate clothes for the family and hair/barber appointments. Jeff coordinates re-enrolling the children in school annually and auto maintenance.

Again, the issue is not whether your spouse can complete the task for him/herself. The issue is whether you are willing to get right in the middle of your marital and familial needs and dirty your hands. Jeff has washed and detangled our daughter's hair to help me, and I have dropped a car off at the dealership for servicing to help Jeff. The objective is to help each other bear the load. Being determined to serve in ways that are meaningful to our spouses, regardless of whether the task is glamorous or comfortable, is the crux of humility in marriage. When you choose to do it and don't have to be begged, it is a demonstration of your honor for your spouse. Honor is very significant in a marriage and the lack of it

STAY HUMBLE

erodes the entire foundation of the relationship.

If when you hear that I prepared my husband's plate or served him in some way it makes your skin crawl, that's a problem. Remember our earlier chapters; self-preservation tactics in a marriage don't work. Rather, they undermine the marriage. The woman who recognized who Jesus was to her washed His feet with her hair. Some may say, "Well, that was Jesus!" Who do you think Jesus is trying to use to demonstrate His love towards you on a daily basis? Is it not your spouse, the person He joined you to? If the thought of keeping the gas tank full in your wife's car sounds like a major and unnecessary inconvenience to you, there is an issue.

Serving someone doesn't decrease your value. Instead, it shows your humility and maturity. There should be very little you are not willing to do for your spouse short of compromising your integrity, of course. Staying humble and remembering that in choosing marriage, you are also choosing to serve is key. How you choose to go about it may vary but each day, it should be apparent to you, your spouse, children, and others that you honor your husband or wife.

In case you are wondering whether I still prepare my husband's plate, I sure do. I can also say that some of the same women who thought I was silly before are also getting up from the table and doing the same.

One person, in particular, who especially thought I was crazy, recently told me she admires the fact I did it anyway

regardless of everyone's opinion about it. You can do the same. Set your mind on what you will do to honor your spouse and do it regardless of what everyone else does or says.

THE NOOK

Are you enjoying *Marriage is Amazing*? Scan this QR code to continue the conversation on this topic. Join Brandi and Jeffrey on "The Nook" vlog!

Chapter Seven
Money Matters

You hear it all over the media; financial problems are a leading cause of divorce. I disagree. People who operate with a spirit of division, selfishness, control, and manipulation cause divorces because they bring that into their finances. Immature and carnal people play games in virtually any area, not just finances. Immaturity leads to divorce, hence, the importance of starting this book on how to identify a mature person.

Money is neutral, so don't be scared of it or what it could potentially do in a marriage. It's the people in the marriage who are wreaking havoc, not the money, children, jobs, lack

of jobs or any other circumstances. Along with the people, it's also a lack of trust, obedience, respect, honor, commitment, communication, and thoughtfulness that takes a marriage down.

Like any other matter, finances involve a bit of education. Prior to linking your life and finances to someone else, you must both be financially literate and have the same perspective on money. Get into the details. I mean the deep details of your views, upbringing, etc. before you get married. Doing so ensures alignment. You can't walk with someone you don't agree with (Amos 3:3). Here are some things to consider:

1. If you are a tither, you do not want to start a marriage with someone who willingly disobeys God's principles on tithing. (Note, disobedient people are rarely disobedient in just one area. You will likely find other areas where God's principles are not adhered to in this person's life.) Do not invite this drama into your home. If you are a tither, marry a tither. Make sure you both agree on how to calculate 10% of all increase. If you need additional guidance in this area to facilitate a discussion, please review the appendix at the end of this book. Remember – no division. My recommendation is to create a situation where you and your spouse feel comfortable operating shared accounts. If you choose to run your home with separate accounts, consider the principle of division. Make sure

MONEY MATTERS

our spiritual enemy is not given access to your marriage through finances. Many marriages have operated this way successfully, but this only works if a "this is mine and this is yours" mentality is not adopted. Don't forget, marriage is a representation of Jesus' relationship with the church. He has given everything He has to save the church (Ephesians 5:23). Check for any of the following when choosing how to establish your accounts and navigate your finances:

    a. **Lack of trust** – this may be warranted if you've married a completely irresponsible person, but again, let's avoid that on the front end

    b. **Selfishness** – Married people have nothing of their own

    c. **Fear** – the need for separation in finances may come from the desire for an escape plan

Do not sow these destructive seeds into your marriage. They erode a relationship over time and the evidence will be apparent eventually.

  2. Be transparent from the beginning. Submit your credit report and major financial obligations to your partner before you marry. When the person signs up to marry you, he/she is absorbing the burden of what comes with you as well. Be honest and don't hide that $200,000 in student loan debt or that repossession on your credit report that drastically changed your credit score. Kickstarting the marriage with a bunch of secrets that will inevitably come to light is a definite

way to welcome a spirit of divorce into your home.

3. **Do not make financial decisions alone.** If there is to be money that you can spend without consulting your spouse, then that should be allocated and set apart after payday. Everything else should be mutually agreed upon.

4. **Do not use money to control your spouse.** You married another adult. Be smart, wise, and thoughtful, but don't be controlling. For example, if you don't like your wife's clothes, don't try to handle that by using money on other things to prevent her from shopping. Address the root problem, which is the way your wife dresses. If you don't like your husband's friends, don't try to withhold money to prevent him from hanging out with them. Address the root problem, which is the company he keeps. Don't try to use money as an easy fix for harder conversations or as a control tactic.

If you are considering marriage, use this checklist to help you with financial matters before you commit to a future together.

Questions to Ask:
- Tell me how your parents navigated money in the home? (Joint accounts, shared credit cards/loans, etc.)
- What are our thoughts on employment? (One person works, both people work, etc.)
- How do you want finances to operate in your home? (Whose name is on legal documents, who

owns accounts, how are accounts and money accessed, what needs to happen before financial decisions are made, etc.)
- What are your financial "deal breakers?" What makes you feel financially insecure?

Things to review before marrying someone:
- Credit Reports
- Loan Statements
- Mortgages and Titles (especially if this person has been married before as he/she may not have finished cleaning up the finances post-divorce.)
- Divorce legal documents
- Child support and alimony legal documents (men, don't assume a woman does not have financial obligations post-divorce.)
- Pay statements

In going through this process, if you find the person you want to marry is struggling, complaining and altogether doesn't understand why you need the information, chances are he/she has a difference of opinion that will cause major issues moving forward. Don't avoid doing the hard work now or making the hard decision to move on.

**Disclaimer: Do not ask someone you just met to tell you all of his/her financial business. This is something meant for people who are truly considering one another for marriage and have entered the premarital counseling stage.

Chapter Eight
Children

Children are an incredible blessing from God (Psalm 127:3). They can be one of the most amazing outgrowths of a healthy marriage. Prior to marrying, it is extremely important to discuss not only surface matters such as how many children you hope to have and your overall vision for a family but also your guidelines on how you will educate, discipline, and raise your children.

We may not realize just how much our upbringings have impacted us, but your rearing in childhood has affected you more than you may realize. Strategies for discipline,

the manner in which children are treated or spoken to and the general view of parent/child relationships begin in our childhood. We have to go to God's Word to determine what the standard is for our relationships with our children rather than our upbringing. This is especially the case if we were not raised in homes where our parents submitted to the leadership of the Holy Spirit and the Word of God.

From my own experiences, in accordance with the Word of God, the three most valuable keys that have kept me as I've partnered with my husband to raise three children are:

1. My marriage is the top priority, second only to my relationship with God (Ephesians 5:21-32; Matthew 22:37-38)
2. My primary responsibility to my children is teaching them to reverence, hear from, and obey the Lord (Proverbs 22:6; Deuteronomy 4:9; Deuteronomy 11:19; Psalm 78:4)
3. My children belong to God and I am their steward (Jeremiah 1:5; 1 Timothy 5:8)

Have you noticed a theme yet? Success in any area: marriage, raising children, work or anything else, is always going to stem from whether our priorities are straight or not. If I am struggling with spiritual malnourishment, this will exhibit itself in a lack of patience and stamina when parenting my children. If I find myself defaulting to the top of my voice, and I am irritable, I know I need to get closer to

CHILDREN

God because He changes me when I am in His presence. I am more capable of drawing on His strength and not operating on my own when I stay close (John 15:5).

A healthy and successful relationship with my husband is one of the best things I can do for my children. It creates an awesome environment to be raised in, and it provides covering and protection for us all. It honors God. That being said, I make meeting the needs of my marriage top priority. I do not give my children everything at the expense of my relationship with my husband. Boundaries must be set.

Many of us stack our lives so high with duties and tasks surrounding our children that our spouses become our roommates. Our connections with each other become surface, brief, and largely administrative. Do not submit to the status quo in your marriage. People grow apart in a pretty simple way: they stop prioritizing one another and their relationships.

If God can't figure out how to help my children achieve their purpose in life without me running around like a tired, angry chicken with my head cut off, then He is no God at all. David's dad thought so little of him that when Samuel said, "Bring all your sons before me," he didn't even call David in the house. He left him outside with the sheep (I Samuel 16:11). Did that stop David from being the king and becoming a household name even among unbelievers to this day? God Himself saw to it that David's purpose was fulfilled regardless

of his father's lack of recognition and every hindrance Saul presented over the years.

Our children's purposes are safe in God's hands. Though we should do our part to be God's instruments and encourage the gifts and talents He has placed within our children, we shouldn't have unreasonable expectations of them, ourselves or our spouses. We can't forget that the primary reason we are in our children's lives is to establish their foundation in the Word of God and teach them how to stand on their two feet in their relationship with God.

We are leading our children to the Lord so that one day, just like us, they can move into a mature relationship with Him and follow His leading to make an impact on this world. Our relationships with our children are not avenues for us to fix everything that didn't go right in our childhoods. They are also not meant to satiate a desire for "clout" and recognition. It is sad to see the stress and pressure some youth operate under, often at the hands of their parents. Whatever issues we have, we are to submit to the leadership of the Holy Spirit to fix them.

Division in the home cannot be permitted in any fashion. As mentioned in earlier chapters, division invites a spirit of divorce into the home. The Enemy loves to work through whoever he can; this includes children. Everyone in the home can be saved and spirit-filled. Yet, if all of us do not choose to follow the Lord's leading, we are easily susceptible

Children

to negative influences and can be used to break the peace in a home. "Divide and conquer" tactics used by children, which typically start early (under the age of 5) must be dealt with swiftly and definitively to communicate that such actions will not be tolerated. Going from one parent to the next in an attempt to get a different answer is an example of this.

In a Christian home, the husband and father is the head official of the game. He is the chair umpire or "head" referee so to speak. He is ultimately accountable for the game, its outcome, and the safety of the players. He enforces the rules that have been established by the governing body (in the case of our homes, the Word of God). The wife and other caretakers are like line judges. They enforce what has been established within the authority they have been given.

Smart leaders submit to those on their teams and don't make judgments or "calls" during the game. They recognize the expertise of those around them. They also know when to delegate their authority to make sure the best outcomes are achieved. As a result, a husband and wife team will partner together with the husband being ultimately accountable for the game and its players.

Out of reverence and respect for God, the "line coach" or support staff (wife, in-laws, nannies, babysitters, teachers, and others with delegated authority) must be especially careful not to make the job of the head official (husband/father) challenging. It's hard enough to meet the demands

of the game without having insubordinate officials on the field as well. By submitting to one another and working in partnership, we can achieve much greater outcomes for our families.

While managing the day-to-day stress of the parental relationship, we must keep at the top of our minds that we are stewards of God's children. Our children belong to God just as adults who have received Jesus belong to God. As stewards, we have to follow the instructions the owner has given for His property and manage it accordingly.

Some of the liberties parents take in rearing children are completely inappropriate. Contrary to popular belief, if the Lord has given us instructions about a matter through the Word of God or inner witness, then that alone is what you should follow. It doesn't matter how inconvenient or challenging it may be. People in submission to God don't have opinions. They obey the instructions of the Word of God and Holy Spirit, which will never contradict one another.

We should treat our roles as stewards over God's children with the utmost gravity. Early and regularly, we should explain to our children we are subject to authority, and we will not fail them or God in our commitment to following the Lord's leadership. Of course, this means at times, we will be completely counter-culture but that's okay as we were called to be peculiar (1 Peter 2:9). God will in no way give us a pass for assuming His seat of authority in the lives of our

Children

children for the sake of our misguided ideals or conveniences (Luke 17:1-2). God is watchful over His children. This should be both comforting and sobering for us parents (Matthew 18:10).

A final thought concerning children is to accept the fact that your children will have diverse personalities, traits, temperaments, and gifts. God will not seek your approval on the type of children He will send you. He will send you who you need and who needs you, so His purpose and plan for this world will be possible. If I were in the heavenly line to pick children, I would have picked an easier crowd.

Instead, the Lord in His wisdom, sent my husband and me three people to lead, learn from, and grow with. They have served as my mirrors over the years and have shown me just how much more I need to grow and mature. I have had to hold firm to my purpose and calling in their lives and not allow this world to crowd out God's plan for each of my unique blessings and me. You may find children to be one of the most meaningful and challenging opportunities you have ever been given as I have.

Finally, children are an amazing blessing, but as with anything else, they can serve as the perfect distraction leading to unnecessary complications in marriage. Agreement with God's Word on the purpose and plan for children in the home, constant communication, and mutual submission is a sure way to stay in sync as a couple. Stay focused and fully rely on God for the wisdom and leadership you need to care for His children.

Chapter Nine
The Bedroom Ministry

We live in a society in which sexual relationships prior to marriage are common. Unfortunately, sexual abuse and pornography are all too common as well. If you have been involved in sexual activities prior to marriage as a result of your own will or against it, you must take the time to ensure you are fully healed mentally, emotionally, and physically. Tremendous frustration awaits you and your partner if you don't.

We also have to deal with Hollywood taking up residence in our bedrooms. What we are exposed to in movies was

created with 15 other people in the room, just the right lighting, and a whole bunch of make-believe. If you want an intimate sexual relationship with your spouse, it will need to be created in the reality of your daily lives.

Sex is a doorway into a person's physical body, and it also facilitates a spiritual bond. Many people today are dealing with physical and mental issues that are the direct result of demonic oppression transmitted in their lives through sex. Have you ever watched a friend or relative change personalities entirely because of his/her partner's influence? In these instances, sexual intimacy is almost always a factor.

When past sexual experiences are left unattended, they do not go away. They simply stack up over time. You and your spouse will eventually do one of two things: (1) deal with the matter head-on or (2) suffer from the lack of connection. When in a sexual relationship with a spouse who has sexual baggage, you are not only trying to satisfy your spouse, but you are also trying to satisfy your spouse's previous lovers. Spiritually, these sexual partners are joined with your spouse. Depending on the nature of the relationship, so much damage may have been done that the person cannot enjoy sexual intimacy without conjuring up memories of their past sexual partners.

Like any other type of healing that is needed, we have to command sexual healing and allow God to give us specific instructions. You may want to speak with a trusted pastor

The Bedroom Ministry

or trained minister for assistance if you have identified you are in sexual bondage (masturbation, which is sex with self included). Whenever there is a strong compulsion and you feel powerless to control yourself, it signifies demonic activity. You may require deliverance or support. Make sure to partner with a Bible-believing, Bible-teaching ministry, and do not submit yourself to unscriptural "deliverance" practices. Deliverance starts with the sound teaching of the Word.

If you find yourself or future spouse in this situation, don't worry, you are not the first believer who has had to go to God or a man or woman of God for help. The important thing is to identify the problem and address it before it spoils your beautiful marriage. Here are a few warning signs that you may need healing for sexual matters:

1. You are aware of your partner's previous sexual experiences or relationships (regardless of your partner's will in the matter). Of course, if your partner was forced into sexual activities, you will need to be gentle and exercise patience to facilitate healing and a transition to a wholesome sexual partnership. Ensure that the spirits of trauma and abuse are not wreaking havoc in your spouse and home.

2. Your partner is openly sensual while the two of you are not married. Is your partner flirtatious? Does your partner use sexual and suggestive language? Does your partner tempt you to cross established boundaries? If the answer to these

questions is yes, it is a direct sign your partner's mind needs to be renewed. This behavior will carry over to your relationship if you permit it.

3. Does your partner show polarity in his/her approach to you? Are they warm and loving sometimes and extremely cold and aloof at other times? This behavior may have a sexual root and should be discussed.

Assuming all systems are go in the sexual arena, and we are not dealing with any of the aforementioned, then the primary thing to consider is that the bedroom is a place of ministry. Unfortunately, many married couples have turned their bedrooms into a place of obligation. This is likely because the couple has not learned that bedroom ministry tells the story of what has been happening in every other room in the house.

Selfish people bring their selfish desires right into their bedrooms (See Chapter 1). Instead of focusing on what they can do to minister in a healthy and non-degrading way to their spouses, they go to bed with a "what's in it for me" attitude. Consequently, the relationship suffers. Married couples should want to come together physically based on the individual's needs. If weeks and months go by without sexual intimacy, you have to wonder why?

When the bedroom is viewed as a place of ministry, it is transformed into a really comforting and peaceful place. It becomes much more collaborative and engaging than the other areas of the house where "work" is being done. The focus changes from task-oriented to a singular focus – your spouse.

It's understandable that when major changes occur in the home such as bringing home a new baby, there will be a season where healing and exhaustion prevent meaningful sexual relations. However, these are just periods of time, and they shouldn't become the norm. Married couples have to safeguard their bedroom and not turn it into the nursery or living room. The ministry that takes place in a man and woman's bedroom should be unlike what happens in the other parts of the home. If the atmosphere of the bedroom is maintained well, you may experience your body relaxing when you enter it. Your day starts to peel off you as your subconscious becomes trained that "this place is different."

If you permit your bedroom to become a place for fussing, arguing, going to bed angry, watching TV and other mentally draining activities, you will find it hard to minister to your spouse there. The atmosphere in a married couple's bedroom should be protected. It's not just bodies that are supposed to be bare in a bedroom, emotions and mindsets should be too.

Let's think about this practically as we consider all God has for us in our bedroom ministry to our spouses. Right now, if money was not an issue, I could hire someone to cook for my husband, wash his clothes, feed and transport our children, etc. Essentially, if what spouses do for each other

could be accomplished by anyone, what do we have to offer each other that is not easily or lawfully replaced?

The first and primary thing that cannot be replaced is the spiritual authority you have over your spouse. Unless you are trying to override your spouse's will (which is futile by the way), you have tremendous authority when it comes to your spouse and home. This is magnified in a greater capacity if you are the husband or spiritual head in the relationship.

The second way is a very practical one. You can connect physically with your spouse and minister to his/her physical and emotional needs in a way no one else can. True, the coming together of a husband and wife is to produce godly seed. Yet, God being awesome never does anything halfway. He has every intention that you will serve and enjoy your spouse in your sexual relationship.

Instead of using sex as witchcraft (mind control) in a marriage, it should be used to serve. Withholding yourself and intentionally looking to control your spouse through your actions is unacceptable. Women are often culprits in this area by subscribing to ungodly mindsets. Men can sometimes fall prey to overtaxing themselves. They use their responsibility to provide for their families as an excuse to persistently come home tired and disconnected. Again, the bedroom is just a mirror of the other rooms in the house.

Don't have a sexual encounter with your spouse with an itemized list of everything you want and need. Take the

The Bedroom Ministry

time to study and understand your spouse to determine how you can meet his/her needs. For example, if your spouse is experiencing a stressful time in life as a result of work or other obligations, you should already have it in your weekly plan to hit the sack a little earlier and a little more often. You will be amazed by what you can learn and identify in your spouse in the atmosphere of an engaged and active physical relationship. You will also be able to practice submitting to the Holy Spirit. In case you haven't realized it, He will teach you everything you need to know concerning your spouse, including your bedroom ministry.

We can't be lazy and expect great results. It's not just sex; it's service. If you are lazy, I don't think you need me to tell you your spouse is not excited to see you coming. By paying attention to your spouse, not only in the 30 minutes before you want to make love, but all day, you can make your physical times more meaningful.

We also have to consider whether we are being absurd in our demands or expectations for performance. If I've been nagging my husband all day, I shouldn't expect the most thoughtful lover to show up in bed. If a man hasn't found the time to engage with his wife about something other than the kids or some errands he needs her to run, he can get ready for a lack of deposit throughout the day demonstrated in a pitiful withdrawal later. The bedroom ministry is fed by the activities going on elsewhere in the house. All things being

equal, when you are in sync elsewhere, you will be in sync in the bedroom.

A final thought is that the same way strong leaders don't have to demand others to follow, thoughtful spouses don't have to beg or demand their spouses to take care of them physically. If no other issues are getting in the way of the relationship, a man naturally responds to his wife as she ministers and a wife naturally responds to her husband as he ministers. Don't miss out on this opportunity to connect with your spouse by devaluing it or skipping the investments needed for great returns. Sexual intimacy can be one of the most meaningful aspects of your marriage.

Chapter Ten
The Foundation

Do not be so spiritually minded that you are of no earthly good. This can apply to marriages because we often don't take the time to understand the reasons our partners married us in the first place. We know the biblical reasons for marriage, but many people marry because they have expectations of how their lives will change in the natural. It is important to understand what your spouse saw in you to want to marry you. It will be foundational in your marriage and ignoring it could present incredible challenges to the relationship.

Before getting married, I asked Jeff why he wanted to

marry me. I knew I needed to understand this to measure up to whatever deep-seated expectations he had for me. After probing and getting past the initial "surface" responses, I was able to boil everything down to two primary reasons:

1. I demonstrated a loyal, "I won't leave" attitude.
2. I was spiritually strong and would encourage and support his spiritual growth.

You may wonder why it is important to know this. It's because all mistakes and blunders in a marriage are not created equal. Some mistakes in a marriage have a multiplication effect. This means, they cut to the core of your relationship with that individual; therefore, you are eroding the very foundation of your marriage through these actions.

For example, in my case, my husband considers my relationship with God of great importance, and it actually attracts him to me. If I go through a "flaky" season where I dabble in activities not fitting for a woman of God, my husband would be there for me, but deep inside, my actions would tap into a foundational stone of our marriage. The effort required to fix this situation is much greater because it involves his foundational need for a relationship with me.

What is it about you that taps into your spouse's foundation? Here is an example of how we can break it down to get at the root. Let's use an imaginary couple named Mary and John. Mary and John have been arguing more lately because John has been picking up additional hours at work.

The Foundation

John wants to help save more money for a new vehicle the family will need within the next year. Mary is frustrated by the lack of time she spends with John and in her discussions with him, she says, "I just want more time with you."

Although she is trying to express the problem, it is still just scratching the surface. John is missing this so the arguing persists. One day, John decides he has had enough fussing and can't understand the problem, so he tells Mary they agreed they wanted to have a third child, which will now necessitate a larger vehicle. This is what they agreed upon and he is trying to help prepare financially. Mary replies that she is fine with the two children they already have and doesn't need a third one if it means less time with him. John is thinking, "Wait a minute – no third child? All because you have to give up two nights of talking to me temporarily? That seems harsh."

Have you ever had a situation that starts deteriorating fast with your spouse, friend or relative? Guess what? Most likely, someone has a foundational need that is not being met. These times of being out of sync have serious consequences and can *multiply* quickly. If Mary and John were a little more in tune with each other's foundational needs, a situation like this could be avoided or minimized.

It's obvious that there is something about talking to John that means more to Mary than meets the eye. It could be Mary doesn't have many people in her "inner circle" she

trusts with her deepest thoughts and concerns. Perhaps one of the things that attracted Mary to John was that he was a thoughtful listener. Things change in relationships. Mary can't and shouldn't expect John to be endlessly available. However, if John knew where his wife's foundation stones were located, he could more easily collaborate with her to develop a solution that makes sense to them both.

Can Mary and John easily get through this? Yes! However, they first need to understand each other's core needs, the foundation, which is largely tied to why they selected each other as partners. They also need to make sure when their behavior is showing the signs of a crack in the foundation, that they address it head-on and quickly. Can you see how something as simple as this example when left unattended, can easily result in a lot of poor word choices, frustration, and potential bitterness? It's all because they don't understand each other's root problems and the consequences.

Why do you want to marry (or why did you want to marry) your partner? If it's based on the person's physical appearance (he or she is "fine"), I hope you know you don't have a valid reason to get married. Physical attraction can go right out the window for a myriad of reasons. Get to the root of the matter and find out why you want the person you've chosen. Be certain to share what you find special and essential with your spouse. Encourage your spouse to do the same.

Here are examples of foundational statements I have

The Foundation

heard from couples over the years about their partners:
1. **He/She inspires me to be better.**
   - In this case, you need to know what specifically about this person's actions and lifestyle is inspirational to you.
2. **He/She makes me feel secure.**
   - What is the root of the security you feel? Is it finances, spiritual strength, physical strength, overall confidence, etc.?
3. **He/She wants a large family like I do.**
   - Be sure you have defined "large" and are in agreement.
4. **He/She is spiritually strong.**
   - Determine what this person does that makes you think he/she is strong. Is the person not easily moved when challenges arise? Does the person pray for you regularly and you love that? What is it specifically?
5. **He/She is smart.**
   - In this case, we need to know what is intellectually stimulating about this person. Does the person study? Is he/she well-versed on a variety of topics or something more specific.
6. **He/She is sweet and thoughtful.**
   - We need to determine what "sweet" and "thoughtful" means. Is the person connecting to

particular actions such as writing letters, calling at certain times, remembering certain things, etc.?

It's important to be specific with your spouse to clarify what you hope to add to each other's lives. Every person is different. Hence, the earlier statements will mean different things for every couple. Nevertheless, the key is to have an open mind and know we need to be considerate and delicate when it comes to the foundational matters in a relationship.

Since Jeff permitted me to put his business on the street, I am putting mine out here too, as an example. ☺ I married Jeff because:

1. He is the most confident man I ever met. His confidence made me trust that my "achiever" personality would not bother or intimidate him.

2. He is a father to his core. I wanted to have children with a man who would be extremely committed to them out of his own desire and not obligation.

Marriage is a beautiful experience in my life and the lives of many others. It can also be for you. Skip the TV, articles, and latest media reports and ask the Lord to lead you to other strong believers who can support you along your journey. If you are pursuing or protecting a marriage, remember to stay excited (Philippians 4:8). Don't lower yourself to the level of other people's experiences. God is still God and the Word works as we work it. You can absolutely have exactly what you are hoping for and even more (Ephesians 3:20). **Marriage is amazing!**

Are You Ready?

The first step to success in life, including marriage, is submitting to the leadership of Jesus Christ. If you have not given your life to Him, then I encourage you to make that quality decision now. I speak from experience when I say you will not regret loving the one who loved you first (I John 4:19).

PRAYER FOR
Salvation and Baptism in the Holy Spirit

Heavenly Father, I come to You in the name of Jesus. I am calling on You as You have directed in Your Word. You said "whoever calls on the name of the Lord shall be saved" (Acts 2:21). I ask Jesus to come into my heart and be Lord over my life according to Romans 10: 9-10. "That if you confess with your mouth the Lord Jesus and believe in your heart that God has raised Him from the dead, you will be saved. For with the heart one believes unto righteousness, and with the mouth confession is made unto salvation." I confess with my mouth Jesus as Lord, and I believe in my heart that God raised Him from the dead. I'm saved.

You also said in Your Word, that You have a gift You want me to receive. "If you then, being evil, know how to give good gifts to your children, how much more will your heavenly Father give the Holy Spirit to those who ask Him"

(Luke 11:13). I also ask You to fill me with your Holy Spirit. I fully expect to speak with other tongues as You give me the utterance (Acts 2:4). Thank You for giving me the support and power I need to walk out a victorious life in you (Acts 1:8a).

Welcome to the family! **Keep the following in mind as you start your journey with Christ:**

> 1. **God is a gentleman and He will not force you to do anything.** He won't force you to pray, read the Word, mature, or anything else. He has made you a new creature (2 Corinthians 5:7) and changed your spirit to be in line with His spirit. He has saved you and put you in right standing with Him (2 Corinthians 5:19-21). Now, it is entirely up to you to renew your mind (Romans 12:2) and submit to God's will for your life (Romans 8:14).
>
> 2. **If you asked to receive Holy Spirit you have Him.** Don't overthink it. Open your mouth and speak whatever sounds and utterances you have, knowing you may feel awkward initially. Keep praying because God is partnering with and helping you (Romans 8:26-27).
>
> 3. **Find a good church home that both preaches the Word of God and obeys it.** 2 Timothy 4:3-4 says "for the time will come when they will not endure sound doctrine, but according to their own

desires, because they have itching ears, they will heap up for themselves teachers; and they will turn their ears away from the truth, and be turned aside to fables." We are living in a time where many are turning away from the Word of God as authority. Be careful, and allow Holy Spirit to show you who your Pastor and co-laborers are in your local community. Study the Word and let God be true and every man a liar (Romans 3:4, Hebrews 10:25, Hebrews 13:17, Romans 12:4-5, Acts 20:28, Acts 2:42, Galatians 6:1-18, 1 Timothy 5:17).

APPENDIX:
Supplemental Tithing Lesson

If you are interested in exploring the subject of tithing with your spouse in greater detail and need a lesson plan, please consider the following:

Hebrews 7:1-10   Tithe means a tenth.
Deuteronomy 8:18 *And you shall remember the Lord your God, for it is He who gives you the power to get wealth, that He may establish His covenant which He swore to your fathers, as it is this day.*

Note: The purpose of having wealth is to establish our Father's covenant on the earth.

Malachi 3:10 *Bring all the tithes into the storehouse that there may be food in my house.*

Romans 11:16 *For if the first fruit is holy, the lump is also holy and if the root is holy, so are the branches.*

Mark 12:17 *And Jesus answered and said to them, "Render to Caesar the things that are Caesar's,*

and to God the things that are God's.

Psalms 24:1 *The earth is the Lord's, and all its fullness, the world and those who dwell therein.*

PAY CHECK

Gross Pay		$1200.00
Deductions:	Federal tax	$ 220.00
	State tax	$60.00
	FICA/MED	$40.00
	Health Benefit	$30.00
Net Pay	(Take Home Pay)	$ 850.00

The tithe is $120.00 if:

- We believe God is the source of our income and ability to get wealth.
- We believe the entire 100% of our increase is the Lord's.
- We believe we are stewards (someone who manages another's property), and God is the one in control of how wealth moves within the kingdom of God.

Net Pay	$ 850.00
Tithe	$ 120.00
Balance	$ 730.00

Hebrews 7:8 *Here mortal men receive tithes, but there*

He receives them, of who it is witnessed that He lives.

Proverbs 3:6 *In all your ways acknowledge Him and He shall direct your paths.*

The way we acknowledge God is by taking counsel from His Word: Ezekiel 44:30; Proverbs 3:9, 10; Luke 6:38; Proverbs 28:27; Ecclesiastes 11:1-6 and 2 Corinthians 9:6-10.

PROMISES FOR TITHERS
(Malachi 3:10-12; Proverbs 3:10)

1. God promised to open the windows of heaven and pour out such a blessing for you there will not be room enough to receive.

2. God promised He would rebuke the devourer for your sakes, so the Devil will not destroy the fruit of your ground.

3. God promised our vines shall bear fruit for us in the field in its season.

4. God promised all nations shall call us blessed.

5. God promised we will be a delightful land.

ABOUT THE *Author*

Brandi M. Stover

Brandi is a licensed facilitator, public speaker, author and entrepreneur. Trumping all titles are her personal favorites, wife and mother. Whether in a classroom or casual conversation, Brandi pursues her purpose to encourage and empower others.

Brandi holds a Bachelors in Business Management and a Masters of Education from NC State University. Having successfully completed her degree requirements, Brandi looks expectantly towards her May 2020 graduation where she will receive her Masters in Christian Ministry.

Visit mishayenterprises.com to connect with Brandi.

www.ingramcontent.com/pod-product-compliance
Lightning Source LLC
Chambersburg PA
CBHW032024040426
42448CB00006B/712